Vic Yelps

by Giulia Verzariu
illustrated by Rusty Fletcher

Decodable 13

McGraw Hill Education

Bothell, WA • Chicago, IL • Columbus, OH • New York, NY

MHEonline.com

McGraw-Hill Education

Send all inquiries to:
McGraw-Hill Education
8787 Orion Place
Columbus, OH 43240

ISBN: 978-0-02-145593-5
MHID: 0-02-145593-7

Printed in China

9 10 11 12 13 DSS 28 27 26 25 24

Vic was in mud.

Yelp!

Yelp!

Jen and Val were glad to help.

Get in the van, Vic.

Jump!

Vic was not in the van yet.

Jen and Val were in mud.

Yes!

Vic is in the van!